AUTUMN
DEVOTIONS

refreshing your soul with
lessons from autumn

by Laura Vae Gatz

CONTENTS

For Jasmine & Joshua who help me
grow more like the Christ

ABUNDANCE

The thief comes only to steal and kill and destroy. I came that they may have life and have it abundantly.

It's late summer or early autumn and my garden is bursting with produce. The warm and sunny temperatures during the day tell me it is still summer but the coolness overnight makes me feel as if autumn is already here. My lettuces are full and the younger plants haven't bolted yet. Surprisingly, the green beans are still producing well into September. I'm still finding cucumbers hidden underneath large leaves, and the cherry tomato bush is loaded with beautiful crimson red cherry sized tomatoes begging to be picked. The melons are all getting ripe and I've begun turning them each day so none will develop a soft spot.

Each trip to my garden yields more homegrown goodness than I can carry back to the house with me in one trip so I've started bringing bigger and bigger baskets out with me. I'm overwhelmed with fresh vegetables and a bit daunted by the hours of canning and freezing ahead of me. How amazing to think that tiny seeds, smaller than a sesame seed, could grow into such healthy and productive plants. All this abundance reminds me of Matthew 13:8, "Other seeds fell on good soil and produced grain, some a hundredfold, some sixty, some thirty."

The end of gardening season is when so many fruits and vegetables are ripe for harvest. As I carry freshly picked goodness into the house, knowing that none of it has been sprayed with pesticides or genetically altered, I am reminded of God's abundance, and not just in how He provides for me. This bountiful garden mirrors the multitude of blessings that God showers on His believers. Although there are different seasons in life, seasons of abundance and seasons of scarcity, God always provides what I need. Of course, what I need isn't always what I want, but it is what God has determined is best for me at that time. I just have to search for God's will for my life, and embrace it. No matter the challenge at hand, God has a plan for my life and is there to protect me, no matter what.

So often we're too wrapped up in the ebb and flow of this life to pay much attention to how the Lord is providing for us. Make an effort this week to slow down. Take a walk alone and pay attention to the wondrous world that God has created all around us: the birds of the air, the trees that sway in the breeze, the brilliantly colored sky and ever-changing clouds. Notice the little creatures in the woods, patterns of light and dark, textures of bark and grasses. Our Creator God is in all of it. And if you believe that His Son Jesus came to earth as a human to die on the cross as a substitute for us, to take away our sins and reconcile us to Him, then God dwells in you as well, through His Holy Spirit.

Dear Lord, Thank You for creating the world. Thank You for the abundance of beauty and blessings that You bring to my life. When I am outside, help me to be in the moment and notice all You've brought into being. Help me to slow down and notice all the details of this earth. Thank You for the abundance of blessings You bestow on me. And thank You for Your constant and ever present grace. Amen.

WEEDS IN THE ASPARAGUS BED

Then desire when it has conceived gives birth to sin, and sin when it is fully grown brings forth death.

JAMES 1:15

There are weeds in my asparagus bed, and not just a few. It looks as if the weeds are the plant I'm trying to cultivate. Those weeds are crafty little buggers. They grow right in-between the asparagus roots, making it almost impossible to effectively pull them out without disturbing the roots of the asparagus. And crab grass loves to grow in there too. Crab grass has a horizontal root in the ground that connects each plant to the next. It's hard to eradicate because it is almost impossible to get the entire root out of the ground. Clover is similar; it sends out shoots that creep along the ground, sending roots down every few inches. The shoot hugs the ground and is difficult to get a hold of.

Weeds in the asparagus bed are like developing bad habits. At first those bad habits are small and not so noticeable, they may even be easy to break. But before long they've gotten entrenched in my life, I've gotten comfortable with them, and breaking from them can seem almost impossible.

Many of my bad habits aren't inherently bad; they're bad because I spend time doing something that has taken the place of a good habit. For example, my husband and I used to spend time praying together before we went to sleep for the night. Then we started watching a television series on Netflix in the evening. Not an inherently evil way to spend time, right? The problem was that we would watch more than one episode at a time and then we would stay up later then we'd planned. When it came time to go to bed, we would slip under the covers and quickly fall asleep without having prayed together. Worldly together-time had replaced together-time with God. It didn't seem like a problem at first. We were enjoying our time together and really enjoying the excitement and drama of the series. Our desire to find out what happened in each successive episode continued to grow until it exceeded our desire to spend time together getting to know God better. Our little weed with shallow roots had moved in, entwined its roots amongst our own, and started to take over.

I have repeatedly found that many bad habits start slowly. They do not seem like they're bad habits at first, because at the beginning they haven't replaced any good habits. But before I'm even aware of it, that new novel has replaced the time I used to spend reading the Bible, and my new exercise routine has replaced the time I used to spend alone with God in prayer.

I've found in order to keep the weeds down in my garden I have to be diligent about pulling them out or tilling the soil frequently, while the weeds are still small. Tilling keeps the soil workable and makes it easier to remove the entire root so the weed doesn't grow back. Staying close to God by staying in The Word daily and having daily quiet time with God keeps us "workable" and more sensitive to the weeds that pop up in our lives. If we can recognize them early, we can keep them from taking over our lives and distracting us from what is really important.

Dear Lord, Give me awareness of the weeds growing in my life, grant me the desire to pull out the entire root, so I can focus on cultivating a stronger and closer relationship with You. Amen.

AFTER THE HARVEST

Do not be conformed to this world, but be transformed by the renewal of your mind, that by testing you may discern what is the will of God, what is good and acceptable and perfect.

ROMANS 2:12

My garden is almost empty again. Just about everything has been harvested, pulled up out of the ground and added to the compost pile. The beans and peas and tomatoes are all harvested and laid away, either canned or in the freezer. We ate our fresh homegrown vegetables over the summer and now the first killing frost is possibly only days away. The garden plot looks so empty now, but I reflect on the amazing and abundant produce it provided our family during the summer.

What do I need to do now in order to prepare the ground for crops next year? I know that this year's plants took nutrients from the soil and those resources need to be replenished. I have let weeds grow and those need to be tilled into the soil.

After a busy season in our lives we can feel depleted and sense the need for replenishment in our mind, body, soul and spirit. What actions do we need to take in order to fill ourselves back up?

Workers in Europe often take a long break in the middle of the day to gather with friends and family and to rest in the midst of their workday. This siesta refreshes them and gives their minds and bodies much needed rest in the middle of the day – time to refuel. Unfortunately, as Americans, that is not a habit that our society promotes.

What each of us needs to fill up our tanks varies from person to person and can change over time: scrapbooking, taking a walk alone, sitting on the couch with a hot mug of tea, listening to favorite music, reading a book, a weekend retreat. Personal renewal can take many forms. Sometimes I spend time being quiet in God's presence and other times I need a nap or an hour or two with a good book. For those who have small children, five minutes alone in the bathroom can do wonders.

In order for God to use us, we need to be close to Him so we can hear His call, and we need to take care of ourselves so our tanks aren't on empty. Although God can supply all we need for any task, I think He probably has a lot more to work with if we take care of ourselves, which is often hard to focus on when so many other things vie for our attention.

Before your day begins, remember that this life is just a dress rehearsal for the next one. Plan your day from that perspective. Of course there are tasks, which have to get done, but make good habits of reading the Bible daily, praying and spending time alone with your Savior. When you find you've forgotten or have fallen out of the habit, try again and ask God to help you. Like soil in the garden, we each need the right nutrients to be able to produce good and abundant fruit.

What do you need to enrich your soil? Spend a minute or two thinking of a few specific things that would help. Then ask God, your friends, or your family to help keep you accountable to taking action.

Dear Lord, This world can be a mental, emotional and physical challenge, especially when it comes to keeping You a priority. It's also hard to focus consistently to develop God-pleasing habits and to take care of my body, mind and soul. Please work within me to persevere when I fail, to remember that Your love sustains me, and open my heart and enable my awareness to hear Your call when it comes. Amen.

STARRY SKIES

And God said, "Let there be lights in the vault of the sky to separate the day from the night, and let them serve as signs to mark sacred times, and days and years, and let them be lights in the vault of the sky to give light on the earth."

GENESIS 1:14-15 NIV

I find a cool and clear autumn evening is an awesome time to sit back, recline comfortably, and gaze at the starry night sky while bundled up in a warm hat. All those stars in the night sky are simply amazing. When I can retreat to a remote location that has little ambient light, the stars in the dark sky seem like jewels twinkling at me. I love a clear sky over Lake Michigan in the northern part of the state. I have seen some awesome clear and starry nights where the definition of the Milky Way is so vivid I feel like I could reach up and grab it. To think that God created those stars simply by speaking is almost beyond comprehension.

As I contemplate God's awesome power I find myself asking why I have such a hard time trusting Him. I know He can do all things; I don't question that. What I have a hard time with is the unknown. How will God answer my prayers? If I ask for patience, is He going to allow me to suffer through a long period during which I'm waiting for my prayer to be answered? If I ask for perseverance, will He enable me to live through a crisis of health?

I know God gives good gifts to those who love Him, but often from our limited human perspective those gifts can be hard to take. We don't like trials even though it is our trials that develop the best traits in our character, the ones that make us more like Christ. And so we may refrain from asking for what we want or need because we are afraid of how God may answer us. Which is kind of silly, even though it certainly doesn't seem silly when we're in the middle of an issue.

God wants to know our desires and our needs. He knows them already but He wants us to open our hearts and minds to Him, and converse with Him about the details of our lives. Like a concerned parent, He is going to provide guidance and support along the way. God gives us the courage and strength "just in time" for whatever trial is before us. I say "just in time" because I've seen how God truly gives me super-human ability in the face of immense trials. In situations I know I would have failed on my own, He lends me His traits to help me through my current challenge.

When I'm feeling overwhelmed and need to rest in God and seek His peace, I imagine God's hands are large enough for me to nestle safely within them, just like a fuzzy yellow chick can be held within two human hands. Then I imagine falling into those loving hands as the feeling of peace and comfort wash over me. It's a similar feeling to the love and safety I felt as a young child when my mother would scoop me up, hold me in her arms, and hug me to her chest as I wrapped my arms around her back and held on, confident that she loved me and would keep me safe. God loves us like that. Spend quiet time today picturing God loving you and holding you safely within His arms.

Dear Lord, You are my refuge and hope. You comfort me and protect me. Grow my faith and bring me nearer to You so I remember to turn to You first when I encounter a scary time or a difficult situation. Remind me that You will give me what I need when I need it and that You will see me through all things. Amen.

BIRD FEEDERS

Lord, sustain me as you promised, that I may live! Do not let my
hope be crushed. Sustain me, and I will be rescued; then I will
meditate continually on your decrees..

PSALM 119: 116-117

Looking out the window while I wash dishes I see the old dead tree branch we stood up and attached to the corner of our back deck. We've hung several bird feeders on it to feed the birds throughout the winter. This winter has been mild so far, with many days without snow cover, so the traffic at our bird feeders has been slower than normal. The birds can still forage for seeds and other things in the dry grass. But once the ground is covered by a thick blanket of snow, we see a dramatic uptick in the number of birds frequenting our feeders. When times get tough, the birds rely on the food we've put out.

I've seen the same sort of behavior in African mammals during a drought. Many of the safari camps have created watering holes within easy viewing of a raised platform where guests can safely sit to observe the animals that come to drink the water. It is a sustaining source of life for them during times of drought.

As soon as the snow melts in our woods the birds return to foraging for their food. In Africa, once the rains start and the animals can find water elsewhere, they start to disperse, no longer solely relying on the safari camps' watering holes.

We too have to find our source of sustenance during our winters and during our dry seasons. When life is easy and going along smoothly it may seem like we can draw our strength from the things of this world, but once we hit a bump in the road or experience a difficult patch, we no longer feel as if this world meets our needs. I'm guilty of this. I often use the entertainment of a movie or TV series to "fill me up," when all it does is occupy my time for a short period, often leaving me feeling flat once the credits have rolled.

While taking time to relax is important for my health and mental well being, when I seek comfort in worldly things I know I'm wasting my time. Yet it can be so difficult to change my habits of turning to those vices when I'm in search of something to bolster my spirits or mend my soul. Only Jesus Christ can fulfill those longings within me. The things of this world are empty and devoid of any lasting substance of value. They're like the chaff that blows away when winnowing grain; worthless.

By spending daily time in the reading of the Bible, taking time away from my busy life to pray, and devoting quiet time alone with my Lord, God will bring peace to my heart and will mend my soul. Those are also the habits that make me more Christ-like, which is ultimately the goal of this life, to become more like Him in every way.

Dear Lord, I so desperately want to draw closer to You and yet I let my daily life keep getting in the way. Please help me to keep Your perspective on life, to remember that this world is the practice-run, and that my goal in this life should be to strive to be as much like You as possible. Lead me in that direction and give me the perseverance to keep after the things of You, versus the things of this world. Amen.

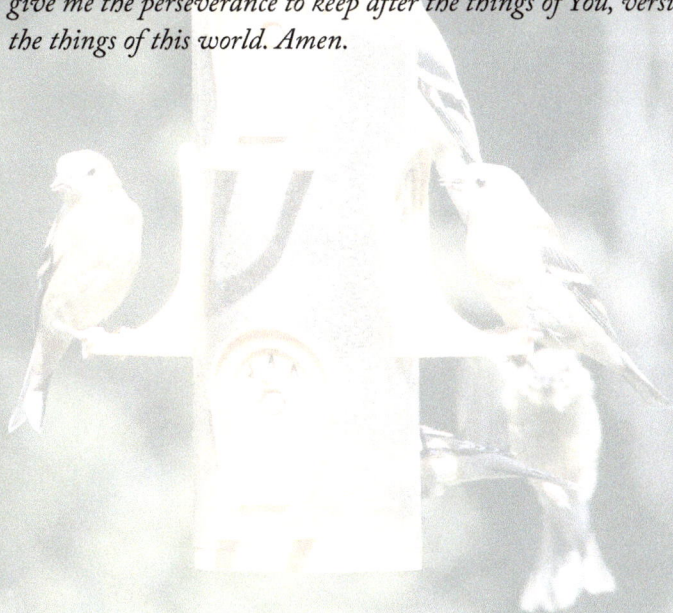

WIND IN THE TREES

The wind blows where it wishes, and you hear its sound, but you do not know where it comes from or where it goes. So it is with everyone who is born of the Spirit.

JOHN 3:8

In the autumn, when the leaves have turned the trees on our dirt road into a colorful canopy, I can hear the dry leaves rustling and rubbing against each other as the wind blows through the branches. A shower of crisp vibrant leaves, falling through the air on their final journey to the ground, accompanies each stiff breeze. I enjoy walks in the late autumn when drifts of leaves invite me to enjoy the age-old fall-pleasure of kicking dry leaves like a child as I wade through the piles.

Once the leaves have fallen off the trees, the sound of the wind in the trees changes. The leaves no longer rustle. Only the branches and tree trunks sway back and forth silently, while the wind makes a lonely sound as if looking for a playmate. Gentle breezes can no longer be heard because they aren't strong enough to move the branches enough to rub against each other.

Even though I can't hear or see the wind, it doesn't mean it's not there. Just like God. Sometimes I feel Him close to me or working in my life; sometimes I don't. But not feeling as if God is there does not mean that He isn't. God is always with those who love and believe in Him. Those are times I just have to believe, to trust that He is with me, that He has a plan, and that nothing can hurt me.

Jeremiah 29:11 (ESV) says "For I know the plans I have for you, declares the Lord, plans for welfare and not for evil, to give you a future and a hope." God is directing my life and has the best in mind for me.

Isaiah 41:10 (ESV) says "Fear not, for I am with you; be not dismayed, for I am your God; I will strengthen you, I will help you, I will uphold you with my righteous right hand." No matter what trial I am in, God is holding me, protecting me and providing for my needs.

As you walk through your day, especially on days when you feel distant from your Lord, close your eyes and picture Jesus walking silently beside you. Feel the support, love, kindness and constant forgiveness that flows out of Him and into you. Know in your heart and in your mind that Jesus loves you and is always with you. He has a plan for you, as it says in Jeremiah 29:11; plans for good and not for evil.

Dear Lord, It can be so difficult some days to feel Your presence. When I am feeling emotionally far from You allow me to picture You walking beside me, providing Your endless love, grace and peace. Grow my small faith to firmly believe that You have a great plan for my life, and that You are working all things together for good for me. Amen.

BORED

Seize life! Eat bread with gusto, drink wine with a robust heart.
Oh yes—God takes pleasure in your pleasure!
Dress festively every morning.
Don't skimp on colors and scarves.
Relish life with the spouse you love
each and every day of your precarious life.
Each day is God's gift. It's all you get in exchange
for the hard work of staying alive.
Make the most of each one!
Whatever turns up, grab it and do it, and heartily!
This is your last and only chance at it,
for there's neither work to do nor thoughts to think, in the company
of the dead, where you're most certainly headed.

ECCLESIASTES 9:7-10 THE MESSAGE

'm bored! And I feel guilty that I'm bored. I do have a lot of tasks that need to get accomplished, but I don't really feel like doing any of them. Looking back on my life I realize I used to be so easily amused. I could get lost in a movie or a book; they'd each take me away to a distant land and I'd imagine myself as one of the main characters, living someone else's life for a few hours. But these days I find it almost impossible to find any sort of fulfillment in a movie or book and I certainly am not able to lose myself in either. It's kind of sad, and I miss being able to do that, but maybe it's also a sign of maturing, just maybe.

Maybe, like Solomon, I've found that everything is meaningless except for God. That thought can make it awfully difficult to care about the everyday duties like getting my work done or planning dinner. And that is when the boredom sets in. I feel overwhelmed with tasks that are seemingly pointless. That emptiness often sucks out any joy I used to get from completing those tasks, because I know in the end, the only endeavors that will really matter are the ones we accomplished for the glory of God.

Why then is it so hard for me to wash dishes for God - to fold the clean laundry for God? When I find myself with a sub-par attitude I have to remind myself that this task does need to get done and I can do it willingly for God and consciously do my best for Him, or I can grumble about it and continue my pity party. When I chose the pity party it does not make me feel any better about life or the task. But other times I say a quick little prayer asking God to encourage me to do this work for Him, and to do my best with a good attitude. And you know what? It works! I feel better about life and the dishes get done with a lot less effort than I felt it was going to take.

Sometimes I'm feeling unsatisfied with life in general which is a more global problem than just getting tired of doing daily repetitive tasks. Dissatisfaction means that my perspective has drifted away from keeping my focus on God and I need to get back on track. This is when I find help perusing my prayer journal. Seeing my past prayers and how God has always been faithful to answer them is reassuring. I am going to add a new prayer to my journal asking that God help dissipate my dissatisfaction and remind me how blessed I am. I will take time to think about and write down the things I'm grateful for and make a list of the blessings God has put in my life. Inevitably these actions lift my spirits, remind me that God loves me unconditionally, has boundless grace to forgive me, and as a result I find a bit of motivation to start being productive again.

Dear Lord, You are the author and perfecter of my faith. Thank You for caring about me as an individual. Thank You for loving me so much that You take time to listen to my whining. Please help me to break free from it. Make Your blessings in my life crystal clear to me. When I feel overwhelmed or simply don't want to do what needs to be done, help me to accomplish those tasks for You with a good attitude and for Your glory. Amen.

CARRYING BURDENS

Carry each other's burdens, and in this way
you will fulfill the law of Christ.

GALATIANS 6:2 NIV

I've been hiking this spring with my husband, Rob. We are training for a several-night backpacking trip later this summer. Let me compare our heights for you: I am 5'8" and Rob is 6'5". He has really long legs and seemingly endless energy and strength. You can imagine just how much faster he can hike than I can. But he likes to hike with me, so he slows down his pace to my own speed. I often feel guilty that I am slowing him down, but he reminds me that the goal is to hike this path together, that he's not walking for speed and he wants to be there to encourage me and help me along the way. It's humbling to accept the love that enables him to slow down to my pace and accept that slower pace graciously.

Rob is also carrying more of our camping gear than I am. His pack is almost twice as heavy as mine is. His pack is so large that sometimes I refer to it as the Green Giant. He's carrying almost everything we need for camping except for our food, my sleeping bag, my air mattress and my clothes. It's certainly an uneven distribution of weight, but by carrying more than I can, he enables us both to achieve our goal. I don't think I'd be able to shoulder a 30 lb pack 50 miles and live to tell about it! But by carrying part of my burden, he is making his burden heavier.

Jesus commands us in Galatians 6:2 to carry each other's burdens. Jesus came to earth humbly as a human to serve others, taking on their burdens as His own. We need to follow His example. Our loving response to loving Jesus is to serve others and carry their burdens.

Shouldering part of the emotional or physical weight of another person's burden doesn't need to be something spectacular like saving someone from a burning building or from drowning. Those opportunities are rare. Look for opportunities to help in a small way, and continue to help.

The Bible speaks of a woman named Tabitha who was mourned by a community of widows that she had ministered to throughout her life. She took on their burdens, making them clothing which would bring them a level of respect, and would also keep them warm. Widows in Jesus's day had a difficult life if they had no brothers or sons to take care of them. Most would live in extreme poverty on the edge of society with no prospects of making a living.

Acts 9:36 says that Tabitha was always doing kind things for others and helping the poor. Notice the word "always." This word implies that her primary focus was on others, and that she persevered in her work. Galatians 6:9 (NIV) supports Tabitha's longevity of support, saying, "Let us not be weary in doing good…"

Dear Lord, Help me to see the opportunities You set before me, and encourage me to humbly serve You today and always by serving others, even when my help seems like such a small thing. Amen.

CHILL IN THE AIR

And God is able to bless you abundantly,
so that in all things at all times, having all that you need,
you will abound in every good work.

2 CORINTHIANS 9:8 NIV

This evening there was a chill in the air for the first time this summer; a foreshadowing of autumn. The crickets sang in the tall dry grass and a few of the less healthy branches of the maple trees are already displaying fall colors. As I strode up the hill past the first farm down the road from my house, my exhaled breath left a cool fog on the lenses of my glasses. There's a small border of leaves building up on the side of the road, blown away from the middle of the road by passing cars. The neighbor's house, which has been hidden from view all summer is now starting to show through holes in the foliage.

Wishing I'd brought a windbreaker to cut the chill, I increase my speed in an effort to warm up. The sound of children playing outside, in the waning light, reaches my ears. It's not long now until pumpkins will be decorating front porches and kids will be walking home from school to the sound of crunchy leaves underfoot.

I'm not ready for summer to be over. It seems like such a brief season. My garden seems empty. When I went out to walk around it looking for produce, there wasn't much left. The tomatoes have all been pulled up, the pea plants long since added to the mulch pile. And even the melon vines have all been gathered up. As my garden empties out, my mulch pile grows. Not only have my plants produced well, they've produced excess organic matter to enrich the soil and replenish it more than they depleted it over the summer.

Autumn causes me to reflect, with gratitude, on the blessings of the year. It's as if the leaves falling off the trees suddenly makes the blessings visible. Blessings are all around me all the time but so often I rush through life, too busy to notice them. This year my garden made me slow down, enough to weed and water it, and tend to the plants as they grew and produced more than I could have imagined. I slowed down in the garden to see the miracle that is the harvest - how one plant can produce so much fruit and at the end of its short life produce a myriad of seeds for the following year.

God tends to us, growing our faith, and enabling us to produce fruit. We plant seeds in those we come in contact with throughout our lives, producing fruit along the way through God's grace. When we come to the end of our lives, hopefully we've planted seeds that will carry on into the next generation, leaving this world a slightly better place for our having lived out our faith in it.

> *Dear Lord, Thank You so much for Your rich blessings in my life. Help me to be mindful of how I impact others. Use me to plant the seeds of Your love and Your grace throughout my life. Amen.*

ENTANGLED

... *"Let us throw off everything that hinders and the sin that so easily entangles, and let us run with perseverance the race marked out for us."*

HEBREWS 12:1 NIV

My husband and I have just started to train for a weeklong hike through Pictured Rocks National Lakeshore, in the upper peninsula of Michigan, that we are planning later this summer. We've started going for walks and hikes with the backpacks we're taking on our trip. The first hike we took was a hilly path through the woods. My pack didn't weigh very much, just 15 pounds, but my muscles weren't used to it and I found myself frequently adjusting the straps, stopping to stretch my aching shoulders and back muscles, and complaining about the myriad of pains I was experiencing.

One of my dreams is to hike the Appalachian Trail some day, so I've read several books written by people who have hiked it. Many start off with huge, heavy packs weighed down with items they think they'll need for their trip. Within the first few days, those hikers realize the definition of "need" changes when they're carrying all their provisions on their back. There are stories of hikers leaving items they've realized aren't necessities, along the side of the trail or in a "hiker box" that can be found at post office buildings close to the trail.

In my life I often carry a mental or physical burden that weighs me down or trips me up: the worry of aging, the fear of declining health, the irritation that arises from having difficult people in my life, the stress of an unbalanced life too focused on succeeding in a career. Sometimes, extra weight comes in the form of bad habits or sin that has crept into my life.

When I find myself spending too much time on the wrong things, not keeping my eye on God through all circumstances, I need to examine what I have in my life that is "extra weight." What in my life I do need to leave on the side of the road? I need to reflect on this question, and ask God,

"What do I have in my life that keeps me from running the course You have ordained me to run; what entangles me?" What gets in the way of my spending time with God? What dominates my thoughts? What hobby has started to take over my life? Hobbies aren't bad, but when they start to distract me from God they may become a stumbling block.

Once I have a good grasp of what is entangling me, the next step is to ask God to help me lay it aside; to help me get back on course; to encourage me to spend consistent time in His presence; to strengthen my faith, and to remind me that He wants the best for me.

Dear Lord, Give me clarity in my heart and a discerning mind to identify the things, habits, and attitudes in my life that entangle me and which keep me from drawing closer to You. Help me to lay aside my personal stumbling blocks. Fill my pack with the fruits of Your Spirit, and help me run this race with perseverance, keeping You by my side through it all. Amen.

HEED THE NUDGE

The man without the Spirit does not accept the things that come from the Spirit of God, for they are foolishness to him, and he cannot understand them, because they are spiritually discerned.

1 CORINTHIANS 2:14 NIV

God sent us His Holy Spirit to guide us. Heed His quiet nudges. They're quiet. They are subtle. But if you pay attention you often will get a sense you are supposed to do something specific. Give into it.

Sometimes when I feel a nudge, I'm not sure if it was my internal monologue talking or the Holy Spirit guiding me, but when I examine the action I feel lead to take and I compare it to who God is, if it is consistent with God's character then I should act on it and act on it immediately. There are so many times that I have listened to that still, small voice, and it was the perfect timing for the person I reached out to. Whether it's the urge to stop and pray for a specific person who just popped into my mind, to call an acquaintance, or write an email reaching out to a friend I haven't contacted in a while, I love that God can talk to us through His Holy Spirit. What an amazing gift that is!

In 1 Kings, chapter 19, when Elijah was running away from Jezebel afraid for his life, he headed out into the wilderness to Mount Sinai to seek direction from God. God sent a mighty windstorm, earthquake, and then a fire, but the Lord was in none of these things. After the fire, Elijah heard a gentle whisper, which brought him out of the cave. Through that quiet whisper, God gave Elijah direction and told him what to do next. When God whispers to us it is an invitation to get personal and have a relationship with Him.

I think that it was in the aftermath of intense occurrences that Elijah was still, and was more attuned to listening for God. He may have been looking for God in the great windstorm and in the earthquake, but he did not find Him there. Once all the excitement had died down it probably made the silence seem all the louder. And when he heard a whisper, it brought him out of the cave where he had been seeking shelter, curious what else he might hear.

What do you do when someone whispers to you? Don't you lean in, and get closer to them so you don't miss anything they say? Have you ever seen what happens when a schoolteacher whispers in her classroom? The children get extra quiet and all side conversations cease.

Isn't it often like that in our own lives? We experience upheaval and look for God in the midst of it, but we don't find Him. God tends to speak to us when we are still, alone, and seeking Him, especially when we are seeking Him with all our heart, as it says in Jeremiah 29:13 NIV, "You will seek me and find me when you seek me with all of your heart." But we need to "lean in" and get close to our Lord. Being apart from others while spending time alone with Him is one way to do that.

> Dear Lord, I want to seek You with all of my heart. Please help me to want to always draw closer to You. Develop in me, the ability to discern Your voice and will for everything in my life. Amen.

FORESHADOWING

So don't worry about tomorrow, for tomorrow will bring its own worries. Today's trouble is enough for today.

MATTHEW 6:34 NLTSE

Autumn is my favorite season, but lately its arrival has been accompanied by a slight sense of dread. Last spring I moved to Michigan and the following winter was especially cold and snowy and lasted for what seemed like forever. There was still snow on the ground in April! Autumn is the foreshadowing of winter. So although I enjoy the crisp, clear, breezy days and the beautiful foliage of the trees, my mind races ahead, worrying about the first snowfall and the long winter to follow. I try to keep myself focused on today, to live in the moment and enjoy the beauty around me, but that can be hard to do when I know what is most likely in store for the next six months.

In Matthew, God warns us to not worry about tomorrow, because tomorrow has enough worries of its own. He wants us to live in the present and let Him take care of all the details. He does not want us to be bogged down by worry. Worry is a sin! Worrying means that we are not trusting God to protect us and keep us safe, nor are we trusting Him to provide strength for the moment. I need to get back to my child-like appreciation of autumn in all of its glory, with drifting piles of crisp leaves to jump in. I need to enjoy today, noticing what is around me right now, letting God take care of tomorrow.

This can be hard to do, especially if you're a planner, like I am. I like to be working a few steps ahead of whatever is going on, so when the future gets here I have a few ideas ready to implement. Once I have a plan I feel in control. But I can't know the future, so planning for it is just a guess, at best. We are surrounded by a society that preaches preparedness, planning and taking action. But God desires our reliance on Him for strength, courage, and the right actions to pursue.

Isaiah 40:31says, "But they who wait for the Lord shall renew their strength; they shall mount up with wings like eagles; they shall run and not be weary; they shall walk and not faint." Because this is a well-known verse it can be easy to miss the beginning. They who what? – WAIT for the Lord. It doesn't say "those that plan ahead," or "those that try to do it for the Lord." Those who wait for the Lord, those are the folks who will have their strength renewed, and the energy they need for the day.

What does waiting for the Lord look like? It can look like different things at different times, but most always will include prayer, quiet time in His presence, and daily study of His Word. When we're all keyed up and worried, those things can be the hardest to slow down to do, but when we spend time in relationship with Him, He will shower us with His peace and patience, and He will renew our strength. So, take five minutes right now to sit on the couch or in a dark room, close your eyes, and tell God that you're taking time to be in His presence. Think of God and his characteristics and ask that He provide the strength you need right now.

Dear Lord, I find it very hard to not worry about tomorrow. Please help me in my weakness and brokenness to find strength in You. Provide the resources and courage I need each day to face the challenges in my life. Use Your Holy Spirit to nudge me, guide me, and enable me to trust that You are in charge, with a plan, and that You will provide what I need exactly when I need it. Amen.

FRUIT

You crown the year with your bounty; your wagon tracks overflow with abundance.

PSALM 65:11

When planning my garden in early spring, I know what vegetables and fruits I want to grow for the season and I plan a garden map of where each kind of plant will be planted. The square footage of my garden dictates how many of each kind of vegetables I will plant. My goal is to plant enough to account for some plants dying, but to also not plant too many. Having more produce than can be canned or frozen also presents a problem. I don't want to waste tasty homegrown vegetables.

Throughout the summer I tend to my plants, ensuring they have enough water, and keeping invasive weeds from choking them or taking their nutrients. I care for those plants, and have to admit sometimes I even talk to them. I take pride in their accomplishments and am overjoyed when they start producing fruit. My husband has witnessed a few happy dances I've performed in the company of my healthy plants.

I am amazed that large, bushy plants grow from miniscule seeds. Some plants start out as seeds smaller than a grain of sand, and end up taller than I am. One of the tomato seeds I planted last year, a cherry tomato, produced hundreds of cherry tomatoes before the frost finally killed the plant. I've never seen such a lush, bushy, incredibly productive cherry tomato plant in my life. Some days were almost comical. I would walk out to my garden to pick these bite-sized tomatoes, and I would return to the house with a large bowl-full of newly ripened tomatoes. Amazing!

The care I give my plants provides a rich environment in which they can grow and produce much. When we spend time cultivating our relationship with our Lord, He too provides a rich environment in which we can thrive and produce much spiritual fruit. The more time and effort we spend getting to know the Creator of the universe, understanding who He is, and understanding His ways, the more we will be like Christ. And the more we reflect the person of Christ, the greater amount of fruit we produce.

I've noticed in my life, during the periods I commit time to studying and reading the Bible, and to spending quiet time in conversation with God, I produce more fruit. What does that mean? The Bible says that the fruit of the Spirit is love, joy, peace, patience, kindness, goodness, faithfulness, gentleness, and self-control. (Galatians 5:22-23.) Those are characteristics of God. The more time I spend with Him, the more I am going to be like Him.

When I spend time with God frequently, I react more lovingly to irritations and inconveniences; I respond more closely the way Jesus would react. When someone cuts me off in traffic, I am quicker to forgive and move on. When lines at the grocery store are long, I make use of my time praying through my prayer list instead of being irritated that the store isn't staffed properly. My perspective changes as I spend time focusing on God, who He is, and how He responded to incidents in His life. Alone, life's stressors put me in a pit by myself, but when I'm in communion with God, He is holding my hand and He pulls me up out of the pit and changes my perspective on life.

Dear Lord, Thank You for sharing the gifts of the Holy Spirit with me. Keep my focus on You and help me bring glory to You in all that I do. Help me see the fruits of the Spirit in my life and help me use them for Your Kingdom. Amen.

PATIO PROBLEMS

More than that, we rejoice in our sufferings, knowing that suffering produces endurance…
ROMANS 5:3

M y husband and I decided it would be nice to have a patio in our back yard, at the base of the stairs that lead down from our back deck. So we planned out what it would look like, picked out the stone, figured out what it would cost, and saved the money we needed to pay for it. Next we started the project, without consulting God. And it has been a challenging lesson to us both. God has certainly used it to teach us a few lessons.

Building this patio has been a huge amount of work, so much more than either of us could have ever imagined, and we ran into difficult circumstances at almost every turn. It's been a few months and we're still working on completing the project. In fact, as I write this I'm taking a rest from the back breaking work of pouring the "grouting dust" into the cracks between the 16"x16" bricks we laid. You wouldn't think that would be hard work, but we have almost 900 square feet of area to cover, and because of the kind of patterned pavers we chose, we have to pour it precisely where we want it, while on our hands and knees.

This project was so much harder than it should have been. When we are completely done with this project I know we can use it as a witness to others about the necessity of asking God for His will in everything we do. We have had the rainiest late-summer either of us can remember. This resulted in the pit we dug being filled with water for weeks on end as we waited for the water to soak into the ground so we could start working again. Much of the hole we dug is comprised of clay which kept that water from soaking into the ground. This led to our purchase of enormous tarps we used to cover our big pit in order to keep the rain out. I could go on and on explaining the delays and hardships we've endured while working on this patio.

We've spent hours working together on this project. We work really well together, and it has been a blessing on a project like this. We've both gotten stronger and in better shape, and I have personally pushed myself far beyond the physical limitations I usually place on myself. This has led to both sleepless nights filled with pain, and a stronger body. We've both had a lot of time to think about God while we've been on our hands and knees. Often we listen to Christian music while we're working. This has helped us keep our thoughts centered on God during the long hours in the sun, working longer and harder than we wanted to.

God has brought good things out of something we did without first consulting Him. He always brings good out of circumstances for those who believe in Him.

It's been a great lesson in patience and perseverance, as well as reminding us that we need to include God in all our plans and to consult Him first. Throughout my life I've seen God's guiding hand, leading me back to Him when I drift off course, teaching me lessons and making me a better, more godly person in spite of myself. His love, compassion and unending patience are almost beyond comprehension and are a shining example of the characteristics we want to emulate.

Dear Lord, You are so awesome in bringing lessons and blessings from the areas in which we did not first consult or ask what Your will was for the situation. Thank You for blessing me with Your insight when I drift off course. Use me to reflect Your love, patience, and compassion to those around me, especially during the trials I encounter in this life. Amen.

HOMEMADE BREAD

People do not live by bread alone, but by every word that comes from the mouth of God.

MATTHEW 4:4

Warm. Crusty. Bread. With butter, of course. Homemade bread, hot out of the oven, emits a mouthwatering aroma that fills our house. I take a pat of real butter and spread it over the steaming slice I've just cut for myself. It melts over the nooks and crannies, enhancing the flavor. Then, the moment I've been waiting for! I take a bite and my teeth encounter that great crisp crunch of crust, encasing a dense, chewy middle. Heavenly! It's wonderful, at least until I've eaten half the loaf and I'm filled with regret over my brief binge and turn to ruminating on what this bread will do to my middle and to my thighs. The temporary pleasure and fulfillment of warm, freshly made bread turns sour once I've overindulged.

I have a tendency to use food to try to fill up that longing in my soul, whether I'm lonely, sad, irritated, or simply bored. I find myself perusing the pantry looking for the next snack that will satisfy me. When the potato chips don't do it, I go back for chocolate covered pretzels. No, that wasn't it. Maybe chips and salsa will satisfy that craving. Eventually I give up and go to bed simply so I won't eat anymore.

In the back of my mind I know I'm not going to find that one food that satisfies me. Food will eventually fill me up, but only physically, not emotionally. When I'm in the midst of my search, I need a bell that rings in my head calling me to stop and turn to God; to turn away from this idol of food, and back to the Maker of all things.

God is the only one who can satisfy our cravings - everything else is meaningless and empty. In Ecclesiastes 1, Solomon, who had asked and received wisdom from the Lord, writes about how everything on this earth is meaningless. He had sampled everything under the sun and had come to the very real conclusion that anything without God is meaningless – like chasing after the wind.

If we seek the Lord with all our heart, we will find Him (Jeremiah 29:13). And all these things will be given to us as well (Matthew 6:33). "These things" refers to food, clothing, shelter, etc. -(Matthew 6:32). See, we have it backwards. We try to fill up our emptiness with earthly things like bread and other snacks which don't work. Once we turn to God to fill up our emptiness, He will fill us with His love, peace and grace. Then we won't have an emptiness to fill – and earthly things will lose their appeal as a means to feel better.

This "turning to God" isn't a one-time thing. It's a continual action in all areas of our lives. If there is an area in your life where you see yourself pursuing things of this world that do not satisfy, give God an opportunity to fill you up. Pray that God would satisfy that longing, and would fulfill your deep desires.

Dear Lord, Thank You for filling me up with Your love. Thank You for being a constant companion by my side even when I go chasing after the wrong things to satisfy the emptiness I find inside of myself. Entice me to turn to You, again and again, throughout my life and in every area of my life. Fill me with Your supernatural peace, love and grace. Amen.

TRAFFIC JAM

Whoever is wise, let him understand these things; whoever is discerning, let him know them; for the ways of the Lord are right, and the upright walk in them, but transgressors stumble in them.

HOSEA 14:9

My husband and I were headed for the train station in Salerno along the narrow twisty roads reminiscent of route 1 along the coast of California at the end of a lovely week relaxing on the mountainous Amalfi coast in Italy. We went from driving smoothly around bends in the road to a standstill within a few seconds. We could see that a large red bus a few vehicles in front of us was having a difficult time passing an approaching bus on the narrow road. For a few minutes everything was at a standstill. No cars moved. The busses didn't move. It was like a faceoff. We joked that eventually the cars coming towards us were going to have to back up or we'd be there all day. We had seen this same situation several times during our stay on the coast when a large bus meets a smaller bus or even a car, along a narrow stretch, and the smaller vehicle has to accommodate the large vehicle, even if it means that car has to convince the line of cars behind him to back up as well. Essentially, the less powerful yields to the more powerful. Most often, the motorcycles and motor scooters will worm their way through to the front of the line and make their way through the traffic jam, and go around the two buses engaged in a stand off.

Our lives can be a bit like those two busses, when we need to yield to God's will. I can be going merrily on my way through life, sailing smoothly around its curves, when I feel God's will leading me in a different direction. And it can take me a while to get on board with the change, creating a standstill for a time.

What it takes to yield to God's will varies from day to day. Sometimes I have to experience my own total brokenness before I'm willing to 'back up the bus' and allow God to control a situation, or my life.

Like the two buses at an impasse, God has all the time in the world and

He wants only the best for us. Our humanness often gets in the way of our being able to wrap our minds around that fact. I have to change my perspective and trust in God in order to yield to His plans for me. All the blessings that He has planned for me just line up waiting until I get on board with "the plan."

Of course there's always the option to completely go around God's will, like the motor scooters that scoot past the large buses, but I don't recommend it! Avoiding God's will for my life has its own lessons, ones I don't care to learn the hard way. Funny how God causes all things to work for good for those who love Him, so even when we're stubborn and do it our own way, God still gets the last word by blessing us in the end.

Dear Lord, Please forgive me when I'm too stubborn to trust Your plan for my life. Remind me, gently, that Your plan is the best possible plan ever, and that You love me and want to bless me more richly than I could ever imagine. Amen.

THE STORM

I awake to the wind and rain hitting the side of the house as if it wants to tear the screens from the windows. Rain hits the siding, sounding like sleet. I'm safe in my bed, but I imagine myself outside in the storm and the feeling that rises in me reminds me of a trial I'm currently working through.

Stress hits like a blast of cold wind, driving stinging raindrops like driving sleet against my face. I feel drowned in overwhelming sadness, like I'm stuck in a place I can't get out of. Hopeless. Helpless. I cry. Why does life have to be so difficult? I ask myself, "How can I deal with this? How will I ever endure this trial?"

Then my husband asks me the perfect question, "Have you asked God to help you through this?" I'm all ready to say yes when I realize that I haven't. That's odd. Why haven't I? I hear the excuses start to bubble up within me, reverberating in my head, even though I haven't verbalized them yet. "Because I didn't think it was something God would be interested in." "Because I thought I could handle it myself." "Because I wanted to handle it myself." "Because I thought if I didn't pray about it maybe it would just go away." But as I hear those thoughts in my head I know they're only excuses, and I don't really have any good reason to not have brought this issue to God.

I'll do anything to make this feeling of helplessness go away, but I'm chagrined that I haven't brought it to the Lord yet. I take time to pray and ask God to give me His strength, love and courage to make it through this hard time. Days pass. I continue to pray about it. I still feel hopeless and helpless. How can I get past these feelings? Have I given it to God or only asked Him to take it away? Sometimes God allows trials in our lives to teach us something. God may not take it away because He knows we will be better for having weathered the storm. What am I to learn from this difficult time?

The next morning I listen to the podcast of a well known Christian speaker while I am stretching. He states that the best stress buster is to just start praising the Lord for who He is and for all He has done. I try it. It really seems to help. Even if I don't feel thankful, the simple act of saying the words, and thinking through what I'm thankful about, redirects my thoughts away from my hopelessness and refocuses them on the awesomeness of God. How powerful, all knowing, all loving, all caring our Heavenly Father is. It's hard to feel powerless when I'm praising the Creator of the Universe, who loves me, and cares about all my needs and concerns.

My internal battle isn't over. I'm still distressed. I'm still sad. But I know I have God on my side. He is with me always, even to the end of the age. It's hard to grasp that, to really and truly get it. During those brief moments that I think I get it, I envision God's constant love like a cushioned safety net of His loving arms that are with me wherever I go. And I also envision a God who is constantly aware of what I'm going through, who has a plan for my life, and a plan for good. No matter what I'm in the middle of, He will bring good out of it. I may not like how it feels at the moment, but if I can keep those thoughts in mind and in my heart, I know that I'll be ok.

Dear Lord, Your ways are so much higher than my ways, and Your thoughts so much higher, and from a completely different perspective, than my thoughts. Help me to not only pray to You about all my concerns, but to leave them with You, confident that You have a plan, that You'll keep me safe, and will bring me out the other side of my trials, stronger and with deeper faith. Give me the knowledge that You are with me each step of the way. Take my fear away, and help me to focus on today. Amen.

GETTING TO KNOW YOU

So I say, let the Holy Spirit guide your lives. Then you won't be doing what your sinful nature craves.
GALATIANS 5:16 NLT

When I was single and in my twenties I remember my mother telling me that she could usually tell when I was dating someone new. When I asked her how, she said she noticed my personality would change a little: a change in my laugh, new ways of phrasing things or an interest in new activities. If my new beau used a particular phrase frequently, it probably started showing up in my conversations. I believe I made these changes unconsciously, "trying on" that new person and some of their attributes, like a pair or pants, to see how they fit.

Married couples in harmonious relationships do this without thinking about it. When two people spend a lot of time together they will often rub off on each other especially if they admire and respect each other. The two become more alike. Personally, I have become tidier because my husband is very neat. I've observed how he unloads the dishwasher as soon as the dishes are clean and I follow suit. Worn coats once taken off are hung back up in the coat closet immediately. And the bathroom counter is free of frequently used items. Because we walk this life together so closely and are so often in each other's presence, I've become a bit more like my husband, and I'm the better for it.

The same is true when we spend time in the Holy Spirit's presence. As a Christ follower, God has gifted me with His Spirit's indwelling presence. That means that the Holy Spirit has taken up residence inside of me. Galatians 5:17 says that we should let the Holy Spirit guide our lives so that we won't do what our sinful nature craves. I have a choice how much time I want to spend with Him, walking in His ways. The Spirit has a whole host of characteristics that are not naturally a part of my sinful nature:

love, joy, peace, patience, kindness, goodness, faithfulness, gentleness and self-control. These gifts are not resident in me but in the Spirit. I am able to take advantage of, and incorporate them into my day by spending time with the Holy Spirit. The more time we spend together the more "like the Christ" I will become.

There are many ways to walk closely with the Spirit. It is much like spending quality time with a friend. I can talk with God as I take a walk, spending time with Him discussing a problem and just letting Him know what is going on in my life. He already knows, but like any friend, He still wants me to confide in Him. Listening to a daily Christian podcast or reading daily devotions keeps me in tune with God and walking along side Him. Small groups and scheduled Bible studies create fellowship opportunities with other believers. Listening as they share how God has worked in each of their lives reinforces my knowledge and understanding of God's great love for me and strengthens my bond with Him.

When my husband and I were first getting to know each other he read a book I authored, in which I described my thoughts, feelings and insights as I traveled around the Southern Hemisphere for two months. After he had completed it, he said he felt like he knew me much better. The Bible is much like that. When we read it we are getting to know and better understand whom God is. The Bible is full of stories illustrating God's characteristics and personality. Reading the Bible daily (consistently) is one way of walking with the Spirit. As we read it we get to know Him better. God will reveal new truths to us each time we seek Him out through His divinely inspired Word.

Dear Lord, I love You so much! Thank You for sending me Your Holy Spirit to live in me and to guide me. Help me to consistently spend time with You. Help me to walk with Your indwelling Holy Spirit so I can take advantage of His many gifts. Amen.

PERSPECTIVE

*Have I not commanded you? Be strong and courageous. Do not be
frightened, and do not be dismayed, for the Lord your God is with
you wherever you go.*

JOSHUA 1:9

God is always in control of my circumstances. No matter what is happening, whether I feel like things are going well, or not so well. I am where I am because God has ordained it. My job is to not be stuck in the past, wondering "if only," and it is to not be worried about the future, wondering "what if?" God calls us to be present in each moment, walking beside Him, holding His hand; not lagging behind and not running ahead.

I find it amazing what happens when I walk in step with my Savior. Situations that could have thrown me for a loop, sending me into a tizzy, have no power over me because I know that God's got it all under control. That peace and freedom open me up to be aware of opportunities to share God's love, with or without words.

I remember when I was young, twisting the chains of a swing so I could twirl in circles, untwisting the chains and then retwisting them to twirl in the opposite direction. If I kept my eyes shut or let the world rush past me in a blur, I would get dizzy and often feel sick to my stomach afterwards. However, if I kept my eyes on one location as I turned, and then quickly swiveled my head to find that same spot, I felt fine afterwards.

When my head is spinning because life is rushing past me, seemingly out of control, if I keep my eyes on God, I avoid a lot of needless pain and unease.

How do I keep my eyes on God and relax, trusting God to carry me through every circumstance? It comes from keeping my focus on Him. That means starting my day talking with Him, sharing my needs and requests, and asking for His help for those loved ones I have prayer requests for. When I need help remembering how He has always been there for me in the past, I visit my prayer journal, reviewing how each prayer request was answered. That history is a powerful testimony to God's faithfulness, and a great reason to keep a prayer journal. Like the Israelites, I often find myself forgetting how God has seen me through dark times and I need a personal reminder of His constancy.

Reading the Bible helps too. It illustrates over and over how much He loves me, how He wants the best for me, how He brings good from bad situations, how He puts people in situations in which they can grow closer to Him and grow in their faith, or they can shine His light into the world.

Praying also helps. It keeps my heart tuned into Christ - thanking Him for specific blessings in my life, thanking Him for His attributes, and thanking Him for His awesome creation. These things cultivate an attitude of gratitude and focus my mind on praise and thanksgiving. It's hard to be irritated, annoyed or upset when your mind and heart are focused on the awesomeness of God!

Dear Lord, Direct my gaze and my focus and keep it firmly planted on You so I don't get dizzy from the blur of life apart from You. Thank You for the tools of conversation, Your Word, and prayer, which You've provided to keep me close to You. Amen.

WAITING AT THE CROSSWALK

Our soul waits for the Lord; he is our help and our shield. For our heart is glad in him, because we trust in his holy name. Let your steadfast love, O Lord, be upon us, even as we hope in you.

PSALM 33: 20-22

While in Seattle, Washington this last week I spent a lot of time walking around the city. I found it interesting that everyone there was remarkably good about not jay walking. The cross walks had a modern system with audible assistance for the visually impaired. If the crosswalk was red the voice would loudly announce "Wait!" repeatedly. When the crosswalk turned green, a loud and quick beep broadcast from the speakers.

I kind of chuckled to myself while waiting to cross the intersection as the crosswalk told me to "wait...wait...wait" because it got me thinking about how God answers prayers and how nice it would be if we could hear a repeating sound, if the answer to our prayer was that God wanted us to wait.

How often in life we don't heed the Holy Spirit's urging and we "cross the road on a red light" anyway, confident in our own ability to keep ourselves safe. We foolishly proceed with our own mission and think we know best. It is so easy to do especially when we're thinking about buying something. It's easy to proceed because we can, without asking God if we should. And even if we do remember to include God in the decision, we may not wait long enough to hear the answer, or assume that silence is equivalent to a "yes," when it might actually be "wait."

Next time you're thinking about how to proceed with a purchase or a decision in your life, remember to pray about it before you make any decisions and then be willing to wait longer than you want to, for His answer. Ask the

Lord to give you clear direction about how to proceed and don't forget to ask for patience while you wait on His timing. I believe, when we are open to it, the Holy Spirit whispers to us, maybe not audibly, but in our intuition, giving us peace when we've made the right decision.

Dear Lord, I want to do what is pleasing to You, and within Your will for my life. Help me remember to include You in all my plans, asking You to make Your will clear to me. Holy Spirit, open my heart and mind to hear Your quiet whispers guiding me. Amen.

POISON IVY

To put off your old self, which belongs to your former manner of life and is corrupt through deceitful desires, and to be renewed in the spirit of your minds, and to put on the new self, created after the likeness of God in true righteousness and holiness.

EPHESIANS 4:22-24

I live on a dirt road on the edge of the country. The sides of our road are covered in poison ivy. It's like an insidious, living, green carpet that extends out into the woods, and up and down rolling hills. It's everywhere. I've never seen so much poison ivy in all my life.

Poison ivy is really hard to kill because the plants are connected by a long horizontal root called a rhizome. Somehow it senses if you've pulled out one of the plants, and compensates by sending another plant up in a different location. So unless you dig down and pull out the rhizome, chances are, the plant is not going to die; it will just keep reproducing and spreading.

Poison ivy can be hard to identify. One plant's leaves can look so different from another plant's leaves. That's how sin can be. It can be tricky to identify the sin in our own lives. And once we've identified it and "pulled it out," another sin can easily take its place.

This winter my husband and I started watching the TV series 24, starring Kiefer Sutherland as Counter Terrorist Unit agent Jack Bauer. Each season of 24 covers 24 hours in his life, using the real time method of narration. It's a fast, thrilling show to watch; one that leaves you on the edge of your seat through each show and at the end of each episode.

Since we'd waited to watch 24 until all episodes had been put on Netflix, we had the luxury of watching as many episodes, back to back, as we wanted. Some nights we would watch 2 or 3. Now, this isn't a sin in and of itself, but when anything, including television, starts to replace other activities that bring us close to God, it can become a sin. Often we found ourselves staying up later than normal, and watching 24 instead of reading our Bible; not getting to bed at a reasonable enough hour to get up early the next morning to spend time alone with God.

Our own personal poison ivy plant had reared its ugly head. We became aware of our bad habit and agreed that once we'd gotten to the end of the series that we would cancel Netflix and stop spending so much time watching TV. We did cancel Netflix but before we knew it, we'd started watching PBS's Downton Abbey. One plant was ripped up, only to be replaced by another.

Unless we can get to the root of the issue, another sin will just replace the one we've just identified and attempted to eradicate. The root of the problem is our tendency to slowly drift away from God without being aware of it. Since we're human we will always be battling sin while we are on this earth, but the key is to not give up the battle; to ask God to help us identify sin and to desire to spend time in the Lord's presence.

Dear Lord, Please help me to be aware of the poison ivy in my life. Help me to see where I am sinning against You by allowing things of this world to replace the time I set aside for being in communion with You. And please grow my desire to be in Your presence. Amen.

DETAILS IN NATURE

And God made the two great lights—the greater light to rule the day and the lesser light to rule the night—and the stars. And God set them in the expanse of the heavens to give light on the earth, to rule over the day and over the night, and to separate the light from the darkness. And God saw that it was good. And there was evening and there was morning, the fourth day.

GENESIS 1:16-19

Autumn energizes me. Crisp days lure me outside to walk and to enjoy the beautiful trees. It is then I notice God's awesome attention to detail in His creation - the myriad of colors in the foliage or the delicate design of flowers. When I think of the interesting animals God created, such as parrot fish, llamas, porcupines, lemurs, etc., with all their unique details and special differences, I realize that if God was interested in the details of creation then He must be interested in the details of my life. He wants to know about each detail so He can have an intimate relationship with me.

How many times have I lost something around the house and looked all over for it but it still eludes me? Then, shortly after saying a short prayer asking God to please help me find this item, (even though I felt a little silly asking God to help with something so inconsequential) I locate it. Those aren't coincidences. The Creator of the universe loves me, and every one of us, and cares about the details of our days. If it matters to us, it matters to Him, and He wants us to talk to Him about our concerns, no matter how small.

No matter how many times I turn to God to help me find something and He helps me, I often find it difficult to fully believe that God really cares about and loves me so much that He wants to know me intimately.

Jesus died a criminal's death on the cross as a substitutionary sacrifice for my sin. God sent His Son to earth to become a human, live a human life, and then die in an agonizing way, so He could save our sorry, sin-filled souls from eternal separation from Him. We find this theme of incredible love throughout the Bible. As I reread the familiar stories of the Bible, I realize how many of them illustrate the love, faithfulness and constancy of God. I believe God intends those stories to speak to each one of us, reminding us how much He loves us and wants the best for us. What an awesome God we have!

Spend some time alone in a quiet and dark place (to minimize distractions). Close your eyes and tell God that you're there to spend time with Him. Ask Him to give you insight into His character. Ask that He speak to your heart and enable you to realize, just a little bit more, just how much He loves you. Then sit quietly, focusing on calming your mind and being silent in the moment, listening for His still, small voice.

> *Dear Lord, You are so awesome and often seem unfathomable. Help me to understand that You love me and want to know me intimately. Aid me in spending quiet time with You often and help me to build that practice into a habit, bringing me into a closer relationship with You. Amen.*

REPETITIVE TASKS

*And let us not grow weary of doing good, for in due season
we will reap, if we do not give up.*

GALATIANS 6:9

Life can feel like a series of repetitive tasks. Sometimes that's all it feels like – Get up, eat breakfast, go to work, exercise, come home, make dinner, and go to bed. Then get up the next day and do it all over again. But many of the things we do over and over again we do because we love someone. We tell our kids to brush their teeth each night. One of these nights they're actually going to remember to do it by themselves, but until that happens, we remind them each night because we want them to grow up with healthy teeth. We remind them to say thank you, and please, to pick up their clothes and clean their rooms and all the things parents do to teach their children manners so they will grow up and be responsible and well-mannered adults.

Coaches experience the same type of repetitive tasks in teaching their students how to play a sport, be a team, and accept defeat gracefully. They instruct the same basics over and over again, year in and year out. It's got to get a little boring, but great coaches stick with it.

Samuel is one of the great Biblical examples of "stick-to-it-ivness." 1 Samuel 7:14 MSG says, "Samuel gave solid leadership to Israel his entire life. Every year he went on a circuit from Bethel to Gilgal to Mizpah. He gave leadership to Israel in each of these places. But always he would return to Ramah, where he lived, and preside from there."

Samuel was called by God to be the spiritual leader of the tribes of Israel. He served his people from the time he was a child until he was an old man. He went from town to town judging the issues of the people, and he did it with integrity. He visited the same towns each year. And he did this over and over, every year. Imagine it. The same route, the same people, the same complaints at each town, year after year. But Samuel was faithful and served his Lord throughout his life.

Sometimes serving the Lord isn't exciting. It can feel repetitive and boring, but if we are carrying out God's will, what we do is important and we need to bring our best selves to these routine tasks, like Samuel did. Being consistent builds faithfulness and perseverance.

Putting this into practice in my own life can be challenging. As I wake up each morning, the long list of things I need to do in order to simply get ready for the day seems so mundane and boring. But if I am to fulfill God's purpose for me on this earth, I need to face the day and do it for my Savior. If I can remember that the "big picture" is eternity, and change my perspective enabling me to realize that perseverance develops faithfulness, and faithfulness readies us for larger tasks in this life; then I am progressing toward God's goal of making me more Christ-like.

Try to think about what God might be developing in YOU as you face the mundane in your life. Realize that He is developing your faithfulness, steadfastness, endurance and character. This life is a proving ground for the next life; we are just temporary residents here. The God-given abilities and talents we develop here will affect the position and responsibility we will have in Heaven.

> *Dear Lord, It is so hard to keep focused on what things in this life have everlasting value. This world seems determined to derail my efforts and keep me off track, enticing me with entertainment and the accumulation of things. Work in my spirit to be able to identify those activities that will produce in me lasting spiritual value, and empower me to keep focused on them. Give me glimpses of Your perspective so that I do not lose hope. Give me the firm knowledge that trials and seemingly mundane tasks in my life are producing everlasting benefits within me. Amen.*

DEER CAMP COMMUNITY

They worshiped together at the Temple each day, met in homes for the Lord's Supper, and shared their meals with great joy and generosity – all the while praising God and enjoying the goodwill of all the people. And each day the Lord added to their fellowship those who were being saved.

ACTS 2:46-47 NLT

On the first day of hunting season, men go out into the woods to sit in silence, patiently waiting for the right deer to wander within range. But although the sport of deer hunting is a solitary sport, once evening has fallen, the tradition in our circle of friends is that our families gather together to share a meal. The dinner on the evening of the first day of hunting season is all about community.

I experienced my first Deer Camp dinner this season and it was just like Thanksgiving dinner. The wives and children of the hunters drive up from their homes and everyone gathers to break bread together. To me it was kind of reminiscent of a barn raising, in which the community comes together to help one farmer erect his barn, and then they all share in a common meal. Everyone works at what they're gifted with – the men with building, the women with making food, and the kids run around forming instant friendships.

This year I decided at the last minute, to drive up and be a part of it. I tossed together a salad and headed up north, meeting Jen, one of the other wives, partway, so we could drive up together. The woman of the house, where dinner was to be held, had been away from home all day, working, and she had wondered how dinner was going to come together. Jen and I brought partially assembled side dishes and finished preparing them there. The man of the house had started the ham in the slow cooker just after lunch, before the hunters headed back out into the cold, to hunt for the second half of the day.

Us women worked together to clear off the table and set it for dinner and put the kitchen in order. We made the food, got it in the oven, and were all the while talking and sharing stories. Community. The kids who hadn't seen each other in months greeted each other gleefully, went outside in the dark to see the horses and ponies and to ride them around bareback, having the time of their lives out on the farm in the dark. Then together they came in to hang out in the family room, giggle, play games, have tickle fights and just hang out.

Dinner came together with a minimum of fuss, and a lot of old fashioned kitchen fellowship. The Lord provided. What a wonderful blessing it was to watch His provision in the making. We all talked and remembered, told stories and tall tales, forming new memories along the way. We departed well after dark, richer for the experience.

The blessings of impromptu community kind of reminds me of how Jesus asked Simon Peter to head back out on the Sea of Galilee to fish (John 21:1-14), during a time when no fish in its right mind would be where Jesus said to fish – and the catch they had was so abundant that it almost sank the boat. In fact, it almost sank two boats! God's blessings can be abundant and unexpected when we open our hearts and minds to follow Him, and what He leads us to do. Trust God to provide and He will give you more blessings than you can imagine.

Dear Lord, You are so abundantly full of grace and love, blessing us immeasurably when we follow Your will for our lives. Thank You for the blessing of community, friendship, and fellowship. You are truly the Author and Finisher of our faith. Amen.

SETBACK

Jesus Christ is the same yesterday and today and forever.

HEBREWS 13:8

've been enamored with hiking the Appalachian Trail for several years. There's just something intriguing about taking off for six-plus months to hike from Georgia to Maine, leaving "normal life" behind, while focusing completely on one enormous task, one day at a time. It "calls" to my wandering spirit. I'm nowhere near fit enough to tackle a challenge like that, and in my mid-40's I may never be, but there is something of the siren song about the idea. As a first step, my husband, Rob, and I are training for a much shorter hike in the Upper Peninsula of Michigan, along the southern edge of Lake Superior – the Pictured Rocks National Lakeshore Trail. We've planned to hike it fairly slowly in honor of my slower pace and have scheduled six days and five nights to hike the 45+ miles.

As part of our training, we've started taking long walks with our backpacks on the roads and trails close to our home, adding weight to our packs each week. This last week my pack tipped the scale at 23 pounds while Rob's is already over 40 pounds and we don't yet have everything in our packs that we'll need during our hike. We're several weeks into our training and last week I was feeling particularly strong and walked farther than I had been while carrying the most weight I've ever carried. Then afterwards we took a 10-mile bike ride, stopping for a coffee drink at the halfway point. All throughout that day I felt great. My confidence has been growing as I see my ability and strength increase. The next day I awoke to a stiff knee and unusual pains. I hobbled around the house for the next few days, alternating heat with cold packs on my knee, and taking anti-inflammatory pills. Nothing helped. I've stretched, I've massaged, and I've elevated my leg and taken it easy. My leg feels good for a short while in the morning and then starts to hurt again as soon as I use it.

After trying everything I could think of to make it better I succumbed to depression and started taking naps in my spare time. It had all been going so well! I'd paced myself so I wouldn't get injured and now all my training seems to have been in vain. It's so frustrating to go from making steady progress to a complete standstill. I've been working so hard toward this goal, not just so I'm in shape when it's time to start our hike, but to improve my health and strength for the rest of my life.

These human bodies of ours falter. They get injured and sick, they age, and they fail us. On days that I'm aching or feeling my age I often imagine what our heavenly bodies will be like and long for the day when there is no more pain, injury, or sickness. It's nice to have that reality to long for, but I need to embrace this present trial, thank the Lord for it and look for His will and His lesson in it.

Experiencing personal weakness gives me an opportunity to contemplate how there is no weakness in my Heavenly Father. He is constant and unchanging, quite unlike our own health or strength. He is always with us and ready to carry us when we are weak, supply sustenance when we are faint, and always be there to love us and encourage us. He often allows challenges in our lives to bring us closer to Him as we search for meaning in the pain, and perseverance in our weakness. When my body falters it is a reminder that I can't rely on it to always carry me where I want to go. Although it is admirable to take care of the bodies that God has given us, my faith should not be in my health or in my physical strength, but in the One who made me. I can take pride in growing stronger and being able to be more active, but I should never forget to thank God for that ability.

I've been focused on strengthening my body and on physical endurance. Maybe the lesson God would have me learn is different than the one I've been seeking. Perhaps the real lesson is that God is the only constant. He is our one unchanging rock on which we should lean and on which we should rely. He never changes and never wanders away from us. He loves us always, through health and sickness.

Dear Lord, Thank You for being my ever present, unchanging strength throughout my life. Thank You for blessing me with a body, and help me through times of sickness, injury and discouragement. Use those trials as times to refocus my faith, reminding me to count on You above all else, and all You provide, instead of relying on my own physical or spiritual strength, of which I really have none – it is all provided by You and Your indwelling Holy Spirit. Amen.

ATTITUDE

"You are the salt of the earth, but if salt has lost its taste, how shall its saltiness be restored? It is no longer good for anything except to be thrown out and trampled under people's feet. "You are the light of the world. A city set on a hill cannot be hidden. Nor do people light a lamp and put it under a basket, but on a stand, and it gives light to all in the house. In the same way, let your light shine before others, so that they may see your good works and give glory to your Father who is in heaven.

MATTHEW 5:13-16

I was flying through one of the airports in the south, where I had the pleasure of encountering a woman who really understands how to be in the moment, and who is unaware of how she blesses others. She is one of the bathroom attendants who keeps the bathrooms sparkling clean and helps keep the line moving along efficiently in one of the Charlotte, NC terminals. She was a bright point in my day. I listened to how she interacted with each woman who walked in. She was full of warmth and sincerity in a place where people usually keep to themselves and interact as little as possible with others. She brightened an otherwise mundane task for each bathroom visitor, in the midst of the rigors of travel.

She made me stop to take stock of my ability to influence others' days. How many opportunities to be salt and light have I let pass me by because I'm focused inwardly instead of outwardly? Probably most of them! But you know, I remember the people who stand out in their positive attitudes. It leaves me wondering what they've got going on in their souls that shines through them to impact my day.

The saying "bloom where you are planted" is right on target with how God commands us to act. God can use every day encounters for His glory. We just need to be available mentally and spiritually. Walk through your day seeking opportunities to give of yourself. It might be as simple as giving a smile to a passing stranger, moving through a crowd with courtesy or simply having the mindset of being helpful. Ask God to show you ways in which you can be of service today. Then listen carefully for that still small voice to guide you. And don't ignore it - follow through on what it says.

Dear Lord, Please open my eyes, ears and heart to the opportunities You place before me each day. Use me to be a blessing to others and remind me to focus on others instead of being so focused on myself. Amen.

STUCK

For as he thinks within himself, so he is. He says to you, "Eat and drink!" But his heart is not with you.

PROVERBS 23:7 NASB

When I am in the middle of a pity party, feeling sorry for myself and bemoaning my present situation, when I change what I am thinking about, my attitude will change. I remember one particular walk when I was wrestling with feelings of extreme dislike and anger towards an exceptionally difficult person in my life. I prayed as I walked, asking God to change my feelings toward that person and I got stuck in my irritation about how their actions negatively affect my family. It wasn't until I decided to stop focusing on the problem and start focusing on God and who He is, remembering the many blessings He has poured out in my life, that my mental attitude changed and I started to feel peace. A paraphrase of Proverbs 23:7 is, "As a person thinks in his heart, so is he."

My husband and I sometimes fall into the habit of making negative comments as a form of sarcastic humor. And we do make each other laugh, but when we stop to examine what we're really doing, we see that it is easy to let negative emotions start to corrupt our hearts. When we identify this bad habit forming we refocus our attention on positive thoughts and change the subject of our conversation.

But there are times I'm not aware of how my negative emotions are affecting others until someone asks me if I'm okay. In my workplace, one of our leadership principles is to be aware of the shadow I am casting. In other words, how are my actions and words affecting others' attitudes? This principle applies to life in general. Not only does negativity degrade the health of our own heart, it easily can affect others negatively.

God wants us to delight in Him. He does not want us to worry or fret. But focusing our energies on the goodness and love of God, our frame of mind can change in a way we couldn't manage on our own. When I'm in my personal pit of despair, this principle doesn't seem like it would work. But it does! By focusing on God's attributes, thanking Him for His love, grace and goodness, my attitude changes. He lifts me out of my self-made pit, because by thinking about our mighty and compassionate Creator, we are drawing nearer to Him, and entering into His shadow.

Dear Lord, When I get stuck in a negative mind set, help me to turn to thoughts of You and Your glorious majesty. Help me to stop casting negative shadows over those I encounter. As I draw nearer to You, make me more like Christ. Amen.

TREE HOLLOWS

*Jesus answered, "Everyone who drinks this water will be thirsty
again, but whoever drinks the water I give them will never thirst.
Indeed, the water I give them will become in them a spring of
water welling up to eternal life."*

JOHN 4:13-14 NIV

There are many mature trees down my road that appear to be fully alive, with a full canopy of leaves each summer. However, upon closer inspection I can see they each have a huge empty hollow right in the midst of their trunk. It's split right open. I wonder how they are able to get enough nutrients from their roots all the way up to their high branches with a gaping hollow large enough for a person to stand in. These trees are putting on a show, when they are really empty inside. They have enough nutrients to look like all the other trees, but their insides are empty. The internal tunnels that lead off of these empty places are great homes for squirrels and chipmunks that like to fill those spaces with nuts and other food for the winter. I wonder if those trees are stronger if they're packed full of nuts? Probably not!

Sometimes I feel like there is a big hole in my middle. I look and act like everyone else, but inside there is something missing. I try to fill up that emptiness with food, entertainment or bad habits, just like the squirrels fill their tree hollows with food, but it doesn't satisfy. Our strength comes from the Lord. Nothing is going to strengthen us like relying on Christ. Only He can fill us up, satisfy, and make us whole.

Jesus found the Samaritan woman at the well, and discovered that she was trying to fill up the hole inside of herself with male relationships. She'd gone through four husbands and was onto another man who was not her husband. Jesus doesn't give her a hard time about this; He simply lets her know that He knows she is searching for something to fill her up. Jesus offers to her His sustaining power, saying in essence, that if she accepts Jesus into her heart, He will fill her up, and keep her full forever. That promise applies to every one who believes that Jesus is God and died on the cross to save us from our sins – allowing each one of us to become reconciled to God the Father.

The hardest part of this message for me is putting it into practice each day as the familiar habits I've developed act like an autopilot, and lead me to rely on myself and the empty comforts of this world. I must practice mindfulness - awareness of the feelings at the root of my actions. What are my longings that drive me? How do I try to fulfill them? If the answer is anything other than with an intimate relationship with my Father in Heaven, then I'm not really accomplishing anything.

Dear Lord, Make me aware of my deep longings, and allow
me to see where I am turning to fill that internal emptiness.
Help me to turn to You for all my needs, in all areas of my life.
Redirect me; fill me with Your everlasting spring of water.
Amen.

DELAYED

Now listen, you who say, "Today or tomorrow we will go to this or that city, spend a year there, carry on business and make money." Why, you do not even know what will happen tomorrow. What is your life? You are a mist that appears for a little while and then vanishes. Instead, you ought to say, "If it is the Lord's will, we will live and do this or that." As it is, you boast in your arrogant schemes. All such boasting is evil.

JAMES 4:13-16 NLTse

Today I had plans to travel down to the Caribbean. The crazy weather across the Midwest changed those plans. I'm so happy that when I awoke this morning I stopped to converse with God. I asked Him to take over today and to allow me to be at peace - going with the flow wherever it happened to take me. So, when my connecting flight cancelled, leaving me wondering how to get to my destination, I didn't freak out or worry about it too much. I still don't know if I'm going to end up at my desired destination by the end of the day, but I have been able, through God's grace, to make the most of the day and keep focused on the present.

I love James 4:13-16, which says in a nutshell that although we may make plans, we really don't know what our brief future holds. God Will should rule our lives and we should seek His will before our own.

I think the Egyptians have the right idea when their response to a question starts out with the phrase "insh Allah" - "God willing." I make plans and often get so upset when they're thwarted. I must remember that wherever I am, that is where God has put me and He has a plan for my life. I need to be open to His plan and keep my eyes open for opportunities to share His love and grace. My mantra needs to be "God has put me here for His purpose. God, keep my heart open to do Your will."

Dear Lord, When my plans don't happen as I'd imagined, please remind me that You have a plan for my life and that

You only want the best for me. Help me to embrace whatever circumstances I am in and stay focused on the present, viewing each challenge as an opportunity You've given me to bring glory to Your Kingdom. Amen.

Walking Together

Since we live by the Spirit, let us keep in step with the Spirit.

GALATIANS 5:25 NIV

One of my favorite daily activities is going out for a walk with my husband. It gives us time to talk, and to catch up with each other when one of us has been traveling and away from home. We walk side by side, sometimes holding hands. Often we'll talk with each other during the whole walk. Sometimes, one of us starts to slip away into our own world, thinking about other things, and we fall out of step with each other, as one of us walks on ahead a few feet. Whoever has been left behind will ask the other to wait up and soon we are walking in sync again.

In much the same way as walking side by side with my spouse or best friend, "Walking with the Spirit" means moving with God, in-step with Him and not getting ahead of Him by doing things on our own or on our own schedule. When we make plans, it's really easy to take action when we want to, instead of first bringing our plans to God to ask if it's His will, and to ask what His timing for us is. For instance when my husband and I decided to build a patio behind our house we went right ahead and built it without stopping to consult our Lord. It wasn't until after we'd started the project and run into repeated problems and delays that it occurred to us that we'd neglected to get God's input on our plans. Through the trials of patio building, I believe God was using our mistake for good, to strengthen our faith, and to help us learn perseverance.

How do we keep in sync with God? We need to make time for Him daily in our lives. In order to walk in step with God we need to be in communion with him, talking with Him, sharing our lives with Him. Jesus Christ seeks a relationship with each and every one of His followers. Jesus sent the Holy Spirit to live in each believer. God's Spirit will lead us as it says in John 16:13, "When the Spirit of truth comes, he will guide you into all the truth, for he will not speak on his own authority, but whatever he hears he will speak, and he will declare to you the things that are to come."

Additionally, the Spirit helps us to pray as it says in Romans 8:26, "Likewise the Spirit helps us in our weakness. For we do not know what to pray for as we ought, but the Spirit himself intercedes for us with groanings too deep for words." What an amazing gift! I can think of innumerable times when my heart was heavy with a request for God, yet I did not have adequate words for it. Praise the Lord that the Spirit intercedes for us!

Walking with God will bring incredible richness to your daily life; it is the best of all walks. And by having the Holy Spirit living inside of us, He will guide us in God's will for us, if we invest time with the Lord, in prayer and in His Word, and in quietness and solitude, seeking the face of God.

Dear Lord, It is so humbling that You would want to spend time with me, and that You know me, my desires and fears, my hopes and dreams. How awe inspiring that thought alone is. Cultivate in me the desire to know You better, to spend daily time with You, and to listen for Your leading in my life. Amen.

BLANKET OF SNOW

*Come now, let us reason together, says the Lord: though
your sins are like scarlet, they shall be as white as snow; though
they are red like crimson, they shall become like wool.*

ISAIAH 1:18

The first accumulation of snow for the season fell today. It fell in large clusters of flakes, straight down. No wind. It's quite a pretty sight from inside the house as well as from outside. During my daily walk outside, I enjoyed my first peek this season at the intricacies of individual flakes, so dainty and fragile. As a clump of snowflakes fell on my dark woolen mittens, I brought my hand up close to my face for a close inspection of each snowflake.

As snow covers the ground it covers a multitude of details: green grass, weeds, those leaves that still need to be raked, water in the wetland, and roads. The landscape becomes more simple, blanketed in white. Snow is winter's gift of future nourishment for plants and trees. It falls on everything. We cannot control it; only embrace it. This can be hard to do early in the season when we're still hoping autumn will last longer, fearful of the long, dark winter.

I love the peace I feel when I finally accept the gift of snow covering the ground. It's beautiful on a calm sunny day, and even glistens in the sun. From inside my cozy home, I feel like Laura Ingalls Wilder, all snug by the fire, safe in my little house, nestled under a warm fleece blanket with a mug of hot tea warming my hands.

Snow makes the world appear simple and clean and reminds me of God's forgiveness. It too is a gift, freely given to those who believe Christ died on the cross for their sins and was then raised to life on the third day. God is able to forgive us all our sins because of Jesus' sacrifice for our sins, for my sins. He took my place and washed me clean so I can be in communion with the Maker of the universe. That's a pretty amazing gift.

God covers our sins like snow blankets a garbage heap in winter. Isaiah

1:18 says, "...though your sins are like scarlet, they shall be as white as snow." And He does this again and again each day, every day. God's grace is constant and ever-present.

Next time you're gazing out the window at a white blanket of snow, think of how God covers you with His love and grace, and as a believer, forgives you of all your sins. Praise the Lord for His goodness and awesome love.

Dear Lord, You are so amazing to have sent Jesus into the world to live as a human and then die a thief's death on the cross to take on all of my sins. Thank You for loving me so much and for Your incredible gift of reconciliation through Christ. You are awesome beyond imagining. Aid me in more fully understanding this gift, and accepting it – realizing that Your grace is a free gift to all who believe in Your name. Amen.

Now that you have finished, share with your friends!

Write a review on Amazon, Goodreads and other book-sharing sites,

and share your thoughts on Facebook.

Thank You!

Laura

ACKNOWLEDGEMENTS

This book is a product of some of the trials God has used as opportunities for growth in my life during the past few years. I've taken lessons I've learned from gardening, traveling, and training for a hiking trip which has not yet been taken, and with His help, distilled God's life lessons and truths into these devotions.

The person who kept me motivated and encouraged throughout the entire process is my husband, Rob. My whole life is enriched because of your ongoing encouragement and love. I treasure living life with you!

And this book would not have been written were it not for my wonderful parents, who poured out their living faith into me from the time I was born. They gave me the firm foundation in Christ from which my faith continually grows.

I praise the Lord for His abundant blessings in my life, and for the lessons He teaches me every day. Thank you Lord, so much, for enabling me to capture, in writing, some of the lessons You have taught me. Please use these devotionals to bless the reader with with Your wisdom and empower them to apply these lessons to their lives. Amen.

ABOUT THE AUTHOR

Laura Vae Gatz was given a camera at a young age, and has yet to put it down. An avid adventure traveler, landscape and nature photographer and writer, Laura travels the world capturing word and visual images of culture, creatures, and the inevitable dialogue in one's head while traveling. A few years ago a friend pointed out to her that she'd traveled to all 7 continents in just 13 months. She's published a dozen coffee table photography books from her travels, available online. In 2009 Laura published a limited edition photo book of a vintage Christian family camp on the shores of Lake Michigan. In 2011 She published *Africa Via Antarctica*, the tales and photographs from her around-the-world, two-month sabbatical. *Beach Devotions* was her first devotional book - available at Amazon.com.

Laura lives with her husband, Rob, in the country on the edge of a wetland, southeast of Grand Rapids, Michigan.

If you enjoyed this book, please consider writing a review at Amazon.com.

www.ingramcontent.com/pod-product-compliance
Lightning Source LLC
Chambersburg PA
CBHW041357090426
42739CB00001B/8